REVELATION
AND RELIGIOUS
EXPERIENCE

BY
JONATHAN WEBBER

© Copyright 1995
First published 1995
Reprinted March 2007

Abacus Educational Services
20 Malvern Close
Worthing
West Sussex
BN11 2HE

ISBN 1 898653 11 9

Other titles available in series:
1. Religious Language
2. The Problem of Evil
3. Faith and Reason
4. God and Proof
6. Life after Death
7. Miracles
8. Science and Religion

Also available:

Ethics series:
1. Ethical Theory and Language
2. Moral Laws
3. Christian Ethics
4. Homosexuality
5. Abortion
6. Euthanasia
7. Environmental Ethics

Also available titles in Fourth Gospel Series.

CONTENTS

INTRODUCTION   4

WHAT IS REVELATION?   5
  Two views of Revelation   5
  Faith   6
  Reason   7
  Difficulties with the propositional view   9
  Difficulties with the nonpropositional
    view   11

WHAT IS RELIGIOUS EXPERIENCE?   12
  Conversion   13
  Mysticism   14
  Prayer   16

ARE RELIGIOUS EXPERIENCES DIFFERENT
FROM ORDINARY EXPERIENCES?   17

CAN RELIGIOUS EXPERIENCES BE
VERIDICAL?   21
  Theological difficulties   21
  Philosophical problems   22
  The Principle of Credulity   26

ARE THERE ANY NON-RELIGIOUS
EXPLANATIONS?   28
  Physiological explanations   28
  Psychological explanations   29
  Is the origin of an experience relevant?   32

IS RELIGIOUS EXPERIENCE EVIDENCE OF
THE EXISTENCE OF GOD?   34

EXAM QUESTIONS   38

WORKSHEET   39

FURTHER READING   41

GLOSSARY   43

INTRODUCTION

This series of booklets has been written specifically to cater for the needs of A- or A/S- Level students of Philosophy or Religious Studies, but may equally be considered a general introduction to the areas debated in the philosophy of religion.

The material in this booklet has been selected and organised with a view to provoking thought and discussion.

WHAT IS REVELATION?

Revelation is divine self-disclosure; through revelation, the Divine becomes known to humanity. Revealed truths are those that could not be accessed by human reason alone and are known only because God has chosen to reveal them (in Christianity, for example, the doctrine of the Trinity is a revealed truth).

▶**Two views of Revelation**

The traditional view of revelation, the **'propositional'** view, is that held by the Roman Catholic church, some sections of conservative Protestant Christianity, Judaism, and Islam. *The Catholic Encyclopedia* (1907-1912), for example, claims that:

> "Revelation may be defined as the communication of some truth by God to a rational creature through means which are beyond the ordinary course of nature ... The essence of Revelation lies in the fact that it is the direct speech of God to man."

On this view, God has revealed certain truths, or propositions, to humanity through the lives of Jesus and his disciples and through the Bible, the authors of which are understood as having been directed by the Holy Spirit. The Bible is therefore understood as "the Word of God". In Roman Catholicism, it remains an open question whether the Bible contains the whole of God's message to humanity or whether there is some essential supplementary knowledge in the traditions of the church.

Judaism is based ultimately on the unequivocal revelation of the Law to Moses on Mount Sinai (Exodus 19-23). Islam is based on the Qur'an, which Muslims consider to be the uncorrupted Word of Allah, having been revealed to the Prophet Muhammad and recorded without error.

This understanding of revelation was relatively undisputed in the Western world until the sixteenth century, when Christian Reformers, most notably Martin Luther, abandoned it. It soon became re-established in Protestant thought, but in the twentieth century, Protestant theology has again set aside the traditional view in favour of the **'non-propositional'** theory of revelation.

According to this view, revelation is not a matter of the Divine imparting knowledge directly to humanity, but of divine action within human history, recognisable in human experience. Theological propositions are not revealed as such, but are the results of human attempts to understand the significance of certain events taken to be revelatory. Revelation, then, comprises both divine activity and human attempts to recognise and understand it.

It is a matter of debate among Protestant theologians whether the events to be taken as revelatory are solely those recorded in the Bible, from the origins of the nation of Israel to the birth of the Christian community (the period of *heilsgeschichte*, or 'holy history'), or whether all events are potentially revelatory since God is always and everywhere active in creation. The fifteenth century Hindu mystic Ravidas, proclaimed the latter view:

> "In every object You are existing all the while. It is my fault
> that I have not learned to see You with my own eyes."

Christians who subscribe to the nonpropositional view generally agree that the Bible is the primary and indispensable witness to the divine revelation which reaches its most full expression in the person of Jesus Christ, whether or not God is recognisable outside the *heilsgeschichte*.

▶ **Faith**

Within the **propositional** view of revelation, faith is the intellectual acceptance of the revealed propositions. The first Vatican Council (1870) defined faith as "a supernatural virtue, by which ... we hold as true what God has revealed ... because of the authority of God who can neither deceive nor be deceived". This understanding of faith as a cognitive assent to a set of truths is denoted by the Latin term *fides*. It requires that faith be attainable by an act of the will, that an individual is psychologically able to decide freely whether to accept or reject the revealed propositions.

Nonpropositional theories of revelation lead to an entirely different understanding of faith. On this understanding, faith is not the acceptance of theological propositions, but consists in *fiducia*—an attitude of personal trust in, and commitment to, the Divine Reality. Faith therefore involves experiencing events as revealing truth about that Reality which ultimately underlies the universe. In a debate over religious language, in the *University* journal 1950-1951, R. M. Hare coined the term '*blik*' to denote a particular way of looking at the world. The nonpropositional view of revelation requires that faith be, in part, a *blik*—a framework within which events are experienced in a particular way. The theory is not that people with religious faith experience the world through rose-tinted spectacles where others see it with the naked eye, but that everyone sees the world through spectacles, all with different tints. Two people with different bliks may experience one phenomenon in entirely different ways. The prophets of the Old Testament, for example, experienced various events in their time as mediating God's intentions for Israel; to see these events as purely social and political, with no divine element, is simply to view them from within a different blik.

The propositional understanding of revelation, then, leads to a view of faith as primarily a form of propositional belief, whereas the nonpropositional view understands faith as primarily an awareness of the Divine from which theological and ethical principles may arise. The propositional view has therefore been criticised for placing too much emphasis on intellectual belief at the expense of personal trust in God. The nonpropositional view, on the other hand, may be criticised for failing to recognise that knowledge about a person is a necessary prerequisite of trust in that person. *The Catholic Encyclopedia*, for example, claims that:

> "it is clear that we cannot put trust in a person ... without previously assenting to or believing in that person's claim to such confidence."

►Reason

The **propositional** understanding of revelation presupposes both that God exists and that God has revealed the truths in question. The Roman Catholic doctrine of *preambula fidei* ('preambles to faith') claims that these suppositions are justified by human reason: the existence of God can be established by philosophical proofs ('natural theology'); acceptance of biblical revelation and of the Church as divinely appointed guardian of revelation are established by visible testimonies such as prophecy fulfilment, miracles, and the growth and durability of the Church. Given this view of the relation between faith and reason, the task of the theologian is to expound and explain the truths of 'natural' and 'revealed' theology, and to systematise these 'facts of faith' into a coherent whole to guard against misunderstanding and misrepresentation.

On the **nonpropositional** understanding of revelation, however, there is no place for 'natural theology', since religiously experienced events constitute the primary source of religious data. The Christian who experiences God as existing and operating in history and in the events of his or her life feels no need for a proof of God's existence. Neither is there 'revealed theology', in the strict sense, since there is no set of truths known to be handed down from the Divine to humanity. The 'facts of faith', on this understanding, comprise the experiential basis of the particular religion, as acknowledged by the religious community (for example, the biblical understanding of the events of the *heilsgeschichte*). The task of the theologian is to explain these 'facts of faith' and to draw out their implications for modern life.

The difficulty with the nonpropositional view of the role of reason is that we are left with no possible method of verifying whether or not a purported revelation actually contains any truth. To appeal to the revelation itself would be to beg the question, and to appeal to any non-revealed knowledge to verify the claim would be to dispose of the need for revelation in the first place. Some theologians, such as Søren Kierkegaard (1813-1855), claim that the truth of revelation is objectively uncertain, and that it is this fact that gives religious faith its value. Others, such as William James in his essay 'The Will to Believe' (1895), have argued that some beliefs, such as Christian faith, are legitimate even without any supporting evidence.

This question does not arise within the propositional view of revelation, where the existence of God is claimed to be established by natural theology and the truths of revelation are, in the words of *The Catholic Encyclopedia*, "guaranteed to us by the infallible magisterium of the church". However, the propositional view has been criticised for its emphasis on knowledge of objective facts about God. Martin Buber (1878-1965), for example, claims that this view leads to a self-seeking and exploitative form of trust in God rather than the personal and nonmanipulative trust required by Christianity.

For further discussion of the debate over the respective roles of faith and reason in religious thought, see booklet 3 in this series: *Faith and Reason*. Aside from this debate, there are a number of other difficulties with each of the two basic views of revelation.

▶ Difficulties with the Propositional View

Modern epistemology (theory of knowledge) undermines the seemingly clear distinction between 'natural' and 'revealed' theology. The distinction relies on the idea that in natural theology the human mind is active in discovering truths, whereas in revealed theology the human is passive in receiving truths. However, the idea that a human mind can passively receive information is widely rejected in modern thought. It is generally agreed that all human knowledge is acquired from external sources by acts of cognition and therefore subject to human limitations of understanding and the particular condition and limitations of the individual concerned. In the first volume of his *Systematic Theology* (1951), Paul Tillich shows the implications of this view for understanding revelation:

> "Since there is no revelation unless there is someone who receives it as revelation, the act of reception is a part of the event itself. The Bible witnesses to that of which it is a part."

If the reception of a revelation is conditioned by the mind of the recipient, there can be no guarantee that a revelation is received or recorded precisely as intended.

Linked to this observation are the claims of modern biblical critics that the biblical writers recorded and expressed their experiences according to their own understanding of the events and with the help of the conceptual and linguistic tools available in the particular place and time in which they were writing. This makes it very difficult, if not impossible, for Christians to identify the original words and actions of divine agency.

Within Christianity, a further difficulty arises from the history of Christian doctrine: some doctrines previously thought to be divinely revealed truths have now been reclassified as human, and even false, opinions. An example of this is the pre-Copernican view that the earth is the centre of the universe around which everything else revolves. If such 'revealed truths' have in the past been reclassified, there seems to be no reason why some propositions, such as that of the Virgin Birth or that of the Incarnation, may not be reclassified in the future. This seems to undermine rational belief in the present status of such propositions as divinely guaranteed facts of faith.

On the propositional view, it would be irrational to deny that a divine revelation contains truth; one can only deny that a purported revelation is of divine origin. Given this, it seems that the correlate view of faith is not assent primarily to revealed propositions, but to the claim that certain propositions are divinely revealed. Moreover, critical sociology reveals that belief systems contain ideological components. Appeal to divinely revealed truths, guaranteed by the infallibility of those receiving the truths, can therefore be seen as a covert way of suppressing doubt and dissent in order to establish a powerful position. It may be argued that the Roman Catholic doctrine of propositional revelation, for example, is a relic of the past, when the church authorities (possibly 'subconsciously') sought to enhance their authority by claiming to be oracles of truth.

The major world religions claim contrary revelations, and some deny the possibility of revelation in the propositional sense. Any organisation based upon propositional revelation is thereby left with the difficult task of attempting to claim credibly that it alone holds the true revelation. The individual is left with the similarly difficult task of deciding which purported revelations are genuine. How is one to choose between the Bible and the Qur'an, for example? Appeal to the claim of the revelation itself (such as claiming that the Bible is divinely inspired because it claims to be divinely inspired) begs the question: if the revelation is not genuine there is no reason to believe its claims. Appealing to a revelation that purports to guarantee certain other ones serves only to add one more revelation to the set to choose from. The only course, then, seems to be to appeal to non-revelatory criteria. To do so, however, would be to deny the need for revelation in the first place: if I can tell by my own senses and reason which revelations are genuine, I must already know the truths that those revelations reveal.

▶Difficulties with the Nonpropositional View

The nonpropositional theory of revelation views theological propositions resulting from revelation as human constructions designed to understand certain events. These statements, therefore, are not considered to be infallible. Given this, there are no difficulties in the recognition that recipients of revelation are active in experiencing and recording events, or in the fact that doctrines may alter. Furthermore, nobody is claiming to be a divine mouthpiece, so there is little or no room for sociological suspicion.

The difficulty of assessing conflicting truth claims, however, remains. If revelatory claims are the products of frameworks of interpretation, (or 'bliks'), it seems impossible to choose between them. Although some bliks may correspond better than others with the way in which the deity intends events to be interpreted, or with what is going on 'behind the scenes', it seems as though the individual cannot possibly know which bliks these are. To choose between frameworks of understanding is simply to judge which corresponds best with one's own. To decide objectively which blik best fits 'the truth' would require privileged access to that truth which, according to the nonpropositional theory of revelation, is not possible.

A further difficulty arises in understanding how it is that a human being can properly respond to events and grasp their revelatory significance. Emil Brunner (1899-1966) claims that there is an image of God (*imago dei*) in the human form that constitutes an innate capacity to respond to divine activity. Karl Barth (1886-1968), on the other hand, insists that human reason is so corrupt since the Fall that humans cannot reach divine truth by means of natural capacities: God has to create a special capacity in the human individual for understanding divine activity. The difficulty with such explanations is that they may seem arbitrary, unverifiable, and suspiciously convenient, and are therefore often considered unsatisfactory.

WHAT IS RELIGIOUS EXPERIENCE?

A religious experience is, quite simply, an experience which has religious significance. It is an insight into usually unseen dimensions of existence which are of intrinsic value and fundamental importance. Such an experience leads to a radical change of outlook and behaviour. In *The Spiritual Nature of Man* (1979), Sir Alister Hardy, who had founded the Religious Experience Research Centre in Oxford ten years earlier, writes:

> "The experience ... [is] quite different from any other type of experience ... it usually induces in the person concerned a conviction that the everyday world is not the whole of reality: there is another dimension to life ... it alters behaviour and changes attitudes ... [and] may be seen by an individual as life-enhancing, or he may recognise it as a special force which gives him added confidence or courage. As a result of their experiences many are led to prayer and religion."

A religious experience may consist in a *direct* experience of the Divine, just as one directly sees a table. Alternatively, such an experience may be *inferential,* such as an overwhelming intuition that the universe is directly dependent on something for its existence, or a strong feeling whilst reading the Qur'an that one is reading divine revelation. (According to the Religious Experience Research Centre, religious experiences are most commonly inferential, triggered by encountering beauty in nature.) That is, as Ninian Smart puts it in *The Religious Experience of Mankind* (1969):

> "A religious experience involves some kind of 'perception' of the *invisible* world, or involves a perception that some visible person or thing is a manifestation of the invisible world."

According to the Religious Experience Research Centre, at least one-third of British people claim to have had a religious experience of some kind. However, no experience entails the existence of its purported object. A dehydrated traveller in a desert may experience seeing an oasis, but the oasis may not exist. The central debate about religious experience concerns whether such experiences are illusory or veridical.

The three main types of religious experience are conversion, mysticism, and prayer.

▶Conversion

The conversion of Saul of Tarsus, later St Paul, in about 33AD, from Pharisaic Jew and persecutor of Christianity, to one of the most significant missionaries in the history of Christianity, is probably the most famous of all conversion experiences. The event central to this change of life was sudden and dramatic:

> "he approached Damascus, and suddenly a light from heaven flashed about him. And he fell to the ground and heard a voice saying to him, 'Saul, Saul, why do you persecute me?' And he said, 'Who are you, Lord?' And he said, 'I am Jesus, whom you are persecuting; but rise and enter the city, and you will be told what you are to do' ... for three days he was without sight". (Acts 9:3-9, RSV).

Not all conversion, or regenerative, experiences are so direct and abrupt. In A Confession (1879), Leo Tolstoy tells of his gradual conversion to Christianity. Having become a successful writer, Tolstoy went through years of depression, feeling that "life is meaningless, vain and evil ... it is better not to live".

> "I would say to myself, 'Well fine, so you will be more famous than Gogol, Pushkin, Shakespeare, Molière, more famous than all the writers in the world, and so what?'
>
> And I had absolutely no answer. ... [I] removed a rope from my room where I undressed every night alone, lest I hang myself from the beam between the cupboards; and I gave up taking a rifle with me on hunting trips so as not to be tempted to end my life".

He searched for an answer to the question "Why do I live?" in science and in philosophy, but found none. His depression deepened until he discovered that "To know God and to live are one and the same thing. God is life." His new-found faith gave his life meaning and ended his depression; "as soon as I recognised that there is a force with power over me I immediately felt the possibility of life."

Tolstoy's experience represents the most common form of conversion experience: a period of depression and despair followed by a realisation that only religious faith provides meaning in life. This realisation, in turn, leads to religious belief and an end to the depression. Whether the religious experience consists only in the conversion itself, or in the depression and the conversion together, depends upon the individual's perception of the events. Tolstoy understood his experience in the latter way:

> "at the same time as I was experiencing the thoughts and observations [that life is meaningless and futile] ... my heart was agonized by a tormenting feeling. I can only describe this feeling as a quest for God."

Conversion experiences are not simply a realisation that there is a dimension of life deeper than that already encountered, but results in a radical alteration in life. William James, in his *The Varieties of Religious Experience* (1902), quotes the words of an American Christian, Joseph Alleine:

> "Conversion is not the putting in a patch of holiness; but with the true convert holiness is woven into all his powers, principles, and practice. The sincere Christian is quite a new fabric, from the foundation to the top-stone. He is a new man, a new creature."

▶Mysticism

A mystical experience is an encounter with the divine source both of all existence and of human salvation. It characteristically involves some kind of sense of the unity of all things in one substance and one life. An *extrovertive* (outward looking) mystical experience is one in which the plurality of objects in the world are transfigured into a single living entity. An *introvertive* (inward looking) mystic, on the other hand, speaks of losing his or her identity as a separate individual and merging slowly into the divine Unity. Of introvertive mystical experience, the Sanskrit religious text *Chandogya Upanishad* (*c*.800BC), explains:

> "As rivers flow to their rest in the ocean and there leave

behind them name and form, so the knower, liberated from name and form, reaches that divine Person beyond the beyond."

Mystics have felt their experiences to be a timeless apprehension of transcendent reality, an imageless rapture in which the mystic gains knowledge of the ultimate truth of existence. Such experiences are considered to be *ineffable*. That is, the content of the experience cannot be precisely described using language descriptive of any other experience and, therefore, cannot be understood fully by anyone who has not had a similar experience. (Ineffability is not limited to mystical experience: consider trying to understand what it is like to experience a migraine if you have never had one.) It is because of this ineffability that mystics tend to use poetic, metaphorical, or even idiosyncratic language to express their experiences.

In *The Varieties of Religious Experience*, William James identifies three hallmarks of mystical experience other than *ineffability*: their *noetic quality* (ie., that they are states of knowledge, not just of emotion); their *transience* (ie., that they cannot be sustained for long); and the *passivity* of the mystic (ie., that the experience is being presented to, and not controlled by, the mystic). Mystical experiences, although passive, generally arise from a course of self-mastery and contemplation. The Christian theologian, St. Bonaventure (1221-1274) divided the experience into three stages: in the *purgative* stage, the mystic is purified and prepared for the experience through meditation; in the *illuminative* stage, the mystic is illuminated both cognitively and emotionally; in the *unitive* stage, the mystic gains a continuing union with the Divine. (The Christian mystic Catherine of Siena (1347-1380) refers to mystical union as 'spiritual marriage'.)

A mystical experience, then, is primarily a total submission of the self to the Divine, in which the mystic becomes united with the Divine and gains an insight into the eternal truth of existence, a truth of immense human importance and upon which salvation depends. Mystical experiences are not simply visions of the divine or any other 'abnormal' spiritual experience: they are unitive, illuminative, and (usually) ecstatic; they are ineffable, noetic, transient, and passive. In the words of Rudolf Otto (1869-1937), a mystical experience is "either a strange fantasy or a glimpse into the eternal relationships of things."

15

▶Prayer

Religious believers, on the whole, not only believe in an invisible, intrinsically valuable dimension to existence, but also hope to have contact with and participate in this reality. A Buddhist monk, for example, meditates to achieve a sense of peace and an insight into the transcendent reality. In the Western religions, the most common form of participation in this reality is through prayer.

Prayer can be considered a religious experience in two ways. The individual's feeling of a divine presence whilst praying, and the relationship that seems to grow between the individual and the Divine through prayer, may be characterised as *internal* responses to prayer. On the other hand, prayers may be 'answered' *externally*, in that a state of affairs may come about, such as a cure for illness, that is understood by the individual to be a response to petitionary, or requesting, prayer. Many religious believers experience 'coincidences' between what they pray for, or are concerned about when they pray, and what eventually comes about. An example of what may be taken to be external answering of prayer is given by William James in *The Varieties of Religious Experience*: the life of George Müller of Bristol:

> "Müller's prayers were of the crassest petitional order. Early in life he resolved on taking certain Bible promises in literal sincerity, and on letting himself be fed, not by his own worldly foresight, but by the Lord's hand. He had an extraordinarily active and successful career, among the fruits of which were the distribution of over two million copies of the Scripture text, in different languages; the equipment of several hundred missionaries; the circulation of more than a hundred and eleven million of scriptural books, pamphlets, and tracts; the building of five large orphanages, and the keeping and educating of thousands of orphans; finally, the establishment of schools in which over a hundred and twenty-one thousand youthful and adult pupils were taught. In the course of this work Mr. Müller received and administered nearly a million and a half of pounds sterling, and travelled over two hundred thousand miles of sea and land ... he never owned any property ... and he left, at the age of eighty-six, an estate worth only a hundred and sixty pounds."

ARE RELIGIOUS EXPERIENCES DIFFERENT FROM ORDINARY EXPERIENCES?

Where sight is associated with eyes, and hearing is associated with ears, there does not seem to be a particular sense-organ, or group of sense-organs, with which one may perceive a divine entity or a religious significance. Similarly, most experiences are easily verified. If I can see a green elephant, and wish to know whether there really is a green elephant or whether I am hallucinating, I can (in principle) ask a rational person, rightly positioned, possessing the requisite faculties, and paying attention, whether or not he or she can also see a green elephant. There does not seem to be any parallel test for religious experiences.

Furthermore, in the case of direct experience of God, there does not seem to be any physical presence. Usually, if I see something (that *is* there), this is because of light-waves moving from the object to my retina; my hearing something is caused by vibrations in the air and their effect on my eardrums. If religious experiences had physical causes, any rightly positioned person with the requisite sense-organs would be able to experience them. That is, assuming that religious experiences such as mysticism or prayerful communication with the Divine are what they claim to be, the synapses of the brain must be triggered by some agency other than the purely physical realm which enables us to see and hear.

Many religious experiences are also claimed to be ineffable. That is, it is claimed that a religious experience (especially mystical experience) cannot be precisely described in normal language.

All this, however, is to say only that religious experiences are *private* experiences. Where many experiences are public (that is, physical in origin and accessible to anyone with the relevant sense-organs), religious experiences are exclusive to a particular individual at a particular time. There are other, non-religious, private experiences. For example, somebody in pain experiences being in pain. Those nearby may be able to see the person's expressions and movements, but they cannot feel the pain. Furthermore, private experiences are usually held to be ineffable: consider trying to describe pain to somebody who had never experienced it. The crucial difference between such 'normal' private experiences and religious experiences is that a pain, or a dream, has no existence beyond the experience of it. The electrical impulses running through a nervous system are not pains, they are electrical impulses; pain is nothing but the experience of pain. A religious experience, on the other hand, is usually claimed to be an experience of an entity that is independent of the experience. Furthermore, 'normal' public experiences have objects that are experienced as located in time and space, but the object of religious experience is not usually considered to be located in time or space.

'Normal' experience is closely linked to our practical concerns. That is, the world is normally viewed in terms of how it can be manipulated to satisfy our needs and desires. Religious experience, it may be argued, is not experienced in terms of its usefulness (or otherwise), but as of value in itself. Such a distinction, however, is too simple. Tolstoy's conversion experience (see pages 13-14), for example, can be seen as rooted in practical concern. Furthermore, aesthetic experience, such as appreciation of music or art, is not usually utilitarian: beauty is enjoyed primarily for its own sake, not for its utility.

'Normal' experience, then, is usually conditioned by our practical concerns, or at least by what we do and do not appreciate. Religious experience, on the other hand, seems to dictate these things, rather than follow them: they alter radically the individual's outlook and concerns, often leading to a change of life.

However, events that lead to a radical alteration in an individual's outlook need not be experienced as religiously significant. The regenerative experience of John Stuart Mill (1806-1873), described in chapter 5 of his *Autobiography*, provides a good example. In 1826, Mill considered whether his aim in life, "to be a reformer of the world", could make him happy, and realised that it could not.

> "the whole foundation on which my life was constructed fell down. All my happiness was to have been found in the continual pursuit of [social reform]. The end had ceased to charm … I seemed to have nothing left to live for."

Mill's depression lasted for six months, until he discovered that:

"Ask yourself whether you are happy, and you cease to be so. The only chance is to treat, not happiness, but some end external to it, as the purpose of life ... and if otherwise fortunately circumstanced, you will inhale happiness with the air you breathe."

Mill's regenerative experience, then, parallels Tolstoy's conversion experience: a period of depression over a renunciation of previous values, ending only with a realisation of some eternal truth or meaning of life. If Mill's experience is seen as 'ordinary', then practical concerns can be created through ordinary, as well as religious, experiences.

If religious experiences have as their object a divine Being, then this object is presumably omnipotent, omniscient, and perfectly free. If this is the case, then the object of religious experience cannot be experienced against that object's will. In Christian terms, you cannot experience God unless God allows you to. This is a marked difference from all other human experiences: a public experience may be had by anyone in the right place at the right time with the requisite sense-organs; non-religious private experiences do not have an external object as such.

Some religious experiences, especially mystical experience, involve an abnormal state of consciousness: in extrovertive mysticism, the mystic's environment is viewed not as a collection of objects but as one living entity; in introvertive mysticism, the mystic loses all sense of individual personal identity. Abnormal states of consciousness, however, are not exclusive to religious experience. They can be brought on by the use of mescaline or lysergic acid diethylamide (LSD), for example. However, mystical experience does not seem to require the use of such drugs.

When an object is experienced, the cultural background of the person experiencing it usually has little or no impact upon the way in which it is experienced. An individual's particular religious background makes no difference to his or her perception of a table. However, an individual's cultural background has an impact upon the way in which he or she understands a religious experience. Mystical experiences, for example, may be described in theistic terms by a mystic raised as a Christian, or in pantheistic terms by a mystic with a Hindu background. It may be argued that the real distinction between the regenerative experiences of Tolstoy and Mill lies in the fact that Tolstoy was brought up within Orthodox Christianity (which he rejected as a young man) whereas Mill was not brought up within a religious framework.

CAN RELIGIOUS EXPERIENCES BE VERIDICAL?

There are a number of theological and philosophical objections to treating religious experiences as experiences of, or caused by, an object of religious worth.

▶**Theological difficulties**

Mystical experience, especially, has been claimed to be contrary to fundamental Western theological principles. In the ninth century, for example, a Muslim mystic (or *Sufi*) named Abu Yazid was so convinced of his union with Allah that he proclaimed "Glory to me—how great is my majesty." Not surprisingly, Islamic orthodoxy considered such a statement blasphemous for claiming the divinity of someone other than Allah. A few years later, al-Hallaj of Baghdad had mystical experiences which led him to proclaim that he was a divine incarnation, and he modelled himself on Jesus of Nazareth. He was crucified for this blasphemy in 922AD. (Islamic orthodoxy is strictly opposed to any doctrine of incarnation.) Islam rejected the possibility that mystical experiences were veridical until Al-Ghazali (1058-1111) proposed that mystical experiences constituted genuine contact with the Divine, but that the feeling of union with divinity is an illusion brought on by mystical ecstasy. Sufism, or mysticism, now has an accepted place in Islam, subject to this understanding of the feeling of union.

A similar theological restriction on the understanding of mysticism was proposed by the Christian theologian Bernard of Clairvaux (1091-1153). In mystical experience, he claimed, the soul remains distinct from God in substance, but the two are united by the flow of grace from God to the mystic and the flow of love from the mystic to God.

A more general theological difficulty with religious experience is that it is not universal: why is it that some people have religious experiences, but others do not? Although mystical experience is thought to accrue from a period of self-disciplinary preparation, the problem remains for other types of religious experience such as prayer and conversion. The English philosopher C. D. Broad (1887-1971) proposed the musical analogy and the blind/sighted analogy to answer this question: just as some people are tone deaf and cannot appreciate music in the same way as others can, so it may be that some people lack the capacity for religious experience; just as a blind person cannot have the same experiences as a sighted person, so it may be that those who do not have religious experiences lack spiritual 'sight'. The central difficulty with these analogies is that it is not clear why the Divine should allow the state of affairs where only some people can recognise religious truths and, therefore, why the shortcomings of some are not corrected.

It may be argued, however, that religious experiences are only to be had by those with a framework of interpretation ('*blik*') within which events may be experienced as religiously significant (see page 7, above). However, such an explanation does not allow for the possibility of a religious experience resulting in a new world-view, or *blik*.

An explanation that evades these difficulties arises from the analysis of human freedom offered by contemporary Christian theologians such as John Hick. If God were obviously manifest, so the argument runs, the only appropriate human activities would be worship and obedience. God is hermetic (ie., hidden), therefore, to allow humans freedom of thought and action. Such freedom is intrinsically valuable because moral and spiritual goals have value only if the agent is free to pursue or not to pursue them. Given this analysis, it is important to point out that prayer is freely undertaken in a spirit of faith, and that most conversion experiences are free acts on the part of the individual. A difficulty arises, however, from such unequivocal 'private revelations' as that experienced by Saul of Tarsus on the road to Damascus: the experience is reported as something that happened to Saul, not as Saul's free act.

▶ **Philosophical problems**

Those who have had religious experiences usually interpret them in terms of a particular religion. However, it is difficult to understand how such an experience can be so precise. A person may feel mystical union with the force underlying the universe, but how is this force to be identified with the deity spoken of in the Qur'an? A person may have an overwhelming feeling of dependence on some greater entity, but why need this entity be the God of Abraham, Isaac, and Jacob? Given that such religious experiences usually lead their subjects to the religion in which they were brought up, or which is dominant in their surrounding culture, it seems as though religious experience cannot yield knowledge of the truth of a particular religion, but at most only knowledge that there is a Divine Reality. It may be that such a discovery compels the subject of the experience to seek a belief-system which best fits his or her experiences.

However, it has been claimed that an experience cannot, on its own, provide knowledge that its object exists. No ontological proposition follows *deductively* from an experience. That is, the fact of experiencing an object does not entail that the object exists. Whilst drunk, a person may experience the room spinning, but it does not follow from this that the room is spinning. It is sometimes argued that an experience of an object justifies an *inductive* assertion that that object exists only if there are agreed tests for distinguishing a genuine experience from an non-genuine one, and if there is good experiential reason to believe that the experienced object is there (eg., whenever I see smoke, something is burning). In the case of religious experience, there are no obvious methods of distinguishing a veridical experience from an illusory one, and many theologians claim that, in principle, there cannot be such a test. Neither are there previous confirmed experiences of the object on which to rely for one's inductive reasoning. However, the principle that claiming that an experienced object exists is only justified by previous experience is problematic. It requires memory of past experiences, but memory-recall is itself experience of an object (ie., a past event); there seems to be no test for distinguishing false memories from veridical ones. Neither is there any possible experiential basis for believing that one's memories are veridical (for such a basis would itself require memory). Furthermore, electrons cannot be sensed in any way; their presence is inferred from events taken to be their effects. If scientists are justified in inferring that there are electrons without any experiential basis or possible test for such an inference, it seems that these conditions are unnecessary.

It has been claimed that religious experiences, unlike 'normal' experiences, are 'self-authenticating'. The experience, so the argument runs, is so overwhelming that it precludes any rational doubt that it is veridical. However, such a claim conflates the concept of correctness with the concept of certainty. The claim that the subject of religious experience is certain that the experience is veridical is not in doubt; one can be certain without being right: a dehydrated traveller in the desert may be sure that there is an oasis in the distance, but this certainty does not rule out the possibility that she is hallucinating.

A philosophical problem arises concerning religious experience as a perception of an immaterial object. Whilst 'normal' private experiences do not have an external object of experience, direct religious experiences are held to be similar to sensory perception. A 'normal' sensory experience is a response to a physical stimulus and posits an object located in time and in space. The object of direct religious experience, on the other hand, is not normally considered to be physical, or located spatially or temporally. If all veridical perception results from physical stimulation, then perceptions of the Divine cannot, it seems, be veridical. However, there seems no reason to accept the principle that all veridical perception is physically stimulated and consequently rule out the possibility that mystical experiences are veridical; mystical experiences, if they are veridical, simply provide a counter-example to the thesis that all veridical perception is physically stimulated. However, it still remains difficult to understand *how* the object of religious experience may be directly perceived.

Recognition of the object of religious experience poses a problem. In 'normal' experiences, we recognise objects that we have seen before and have been told what they are called and what they are (although we may infer this last fact). If an individual experiences the Divine for the first time, how can he or she recognise that object as divine? There do not seem to be any particular properties of the Divine that we are sure of and can recognise. It may be replied that the object of the experience is taken to be divine because the subject experiences it as, for example, all-encompassing and of fundamental human importance. However, this may still be a case of mistaken identity.

Two further problems with religious experience arise from the concepts of finitude and infinitude. In his article 'Visions' (1955), Alasdair MacIntyre writes:

> "The definition of God as infinite is intended precisely to distinguish between God and everything finite, but to take the divine out of the finite is to remove it from the entire world of human experience."

There are essentially two problems with experiencing an infinite object. Firstly, indirect experience of the Divine seems impossible, since something infinite cannot be manifest in something finite. That is, a finite object cannot reveal anything that is infinite because the object itself is finite. This problem, however, can be easily disposed of: most indirect religious experiences are not claimed to be experiences of the Divine made manifest in some particular object, but overwhelmingly powerful feelings that arise when experiencing or contemplating the object in question. That is, the Divine is not experienced but inferred; the finite object is not a manifestation but a sign. The second problem concerns direct religious experiences. A finite mind, it is said, cannot experience an infinite reality, since infinity cannot be contained within the finite. However, it may be counter-argued, for example, that such an experience is not an experience of the Divine as such, but an experience of being in the presence of the Divine. This latter experience has the object 'being in the presence of the Divine', which is not an infinite object.

There is a philosophical difficulty concerning 'external' responses to prayer. This difficulty is parallel to the problem of evil: if the deity is omniscient, omnipotent, and perfectly good, the argument runs, then there is no need for the individual to request anything, since those things that would be good for the individual will be brought about anyway, and other things will not be brought about even if they are prayed for. In response to this, however, it may be argued that if the Divine did control events in this way, then humans would have no freedom and hence no dignity, and there would be no possibility of spiritual and moral goodness (see page 21, above). Moreover, if all good things and no bad things will happen anyway, then there is no point in any human ever doing anything. The Christian philosopher Blaise

Pascal (1623-1662) claimed that "God instituted prayer in order to lend his creatures the dignity of causality", to which C. S. Lewis (1898-1963) added:

> "But not only prayer; whenever we act at all he lends us that dignity. It is not really stranger, nor less strange, that my prayers should affect the course of events than that my other actions should do so."

▶The Principle of Credulity

In *The Existence of God* (1979), Richard Swinburne argues that such *a priori* doubts concerning the nature of religious experience do not constitute a rational way to proceed:

> "Initial scepticism about perceptual claims—regarding them as guilty until proven innocent—will give you no knowledge at all. ... Religious perceptual claims deserve to be taken as seriously as perceptual claims of any other kind."

In 'normal' experience, we tend to trust our senses unless we have good reason to believe that we are being misled; if it seems to me that a certain object is present, I usually take it that the object is present. Not only is this usual procedure, but it also seems to be the most rational. It would be irrational and unhelpful to doubt the existence of the object of every experience. Thus, according to Swinburne, "How things seem to be is good grounds for a belief about how things are." It is from these observations that Swinburne formulates his 'principle of credulity':

> "apparent perceptions ought to be taken at their face value in the absence of positive reason for challenge."

That is, unless there are positive reasons to believe otherwise, it is rational to believe that any experience, religious or otherwise, that posits an external object, is veridical. Reason for believing that an experience is not veridical can be provided either by knowledge that the object does not exist (or was not present to the individual who claims to have experienced it), or by knowledge of the presence of some sufficient cause of the experience other than the object experienced. In the case of religious experience, there is no way of knowing that the purported object either does not exist or was not present, so the only possible reason for denying that the experience was veridical is to discover that some event or object other than that experienced was both present and a sufficient cause of the experience.

ARE THERE ANY NON-RELIGIOUS EXPLANATIONS?

A naturalistic explanation can easily be given for the phenomenon of seemingly externally answered prayers: coincidence. Given the number and variety of things prayed for, and the number of events and states of affairs that come about, it seems hardly remarkable that there may be coincidences between the two. To claim that prayers are being answered, on this view, is like considering only winning bets on horses and claiming that betting on a horse has the power to bring it about that the horse wins the race.

Other religious experiences, however, are not so easily explained away, since there is little doubt that the experiences in question actually happen.

▶Physiological explanations

A physiological explanation of, for example, electrical activity in the brain during mystical experience does not, of itself, provide an explanation of the origin of an event. If I am seeing a table, a description of the workings of the eye, the optic nerve, and the brain, will say nothing about whether there really is a table in front of me.

Research into seismic activity has shown that shortly before earthquakes, tectonic plates shift slightly against one another, producing a massive electrical charge in the air above the surface. Furthermore, many purported encounters with extra-terrestrial beings have occurred at times and places that would have been affected by such a charge. Recent research into the effects this electrical activity might have on the brain of a bystander has shown that the electricity interferes with normal brain activity, which can result in illusory bodily sensations and other experiences. If the occurrences of mystical experiences were to be linked to natural electrical activity in the same way, this would provide a purely physiological explanation of the experience. No such link has ever been made, however, and since mystics sometimes have these experiences in the company of people who do not have them, it may be argued that this link could not be made—unless there is something different about the brain of the mystic.

One early sign of a brain tumour is temporal lobe epilepsy, which can cause hallucinations. Hallucinations can also be triggered by tuberculosis. However, there is little evidence that mysticism is caused by brain tumours or tuberculosis—many mystics had their experiences over a number of years without showing signs of physical deterioration associated with these ailments.

One plausible physiological explanation of a religious experience concerns the conversion of Saul of Tarsus, later St Paul. Paul writes, in his letters, of being weakened by a "thorn in the flesh" (2 Corinthians 4: 10; 12: 7; Galatians 4: 13-14), though he gives us no details of this condition. If this "thorn" were epilepsy, some have observed, then Paul's falling to the ground and being blinded by a bright light could be attributed to a particularly bad fit. However, this explanation does not account for the voice Paul heard or the radical change of life that followed.

▶Psychological explanations

If Paul did have an epileptic fit on the road to Damascus, the voices and conversion may be accounted for in psychological terms: it may be that Paul was delirious and hallucinating, the content of his hallucination venting his subconscious guilt about persecuting Christians. This, of course, is merely unverifiable speculation, but still it may be that religious experiences are rooted ultimately in psychological events.

One psychological explanation of religious experience arises from the observation that inner disturbances are sometimes projected onto the external objective world in such a way that the individual experiences them as external facts rather than as purely mental events. Such a projection need not be as dramatic as the above account of Paul's conversion. It is not uncommon, for example, to hear someone say "that slug is disgusting", believing that the slug *is* disgusting. The slug, of course, is not in itself disgusting; it does not have the property of 'being disgusting'. The slug is just a slug. The feeling of disgust is an internal, subjective feeling projected onto the slug.

The founder of psychoanalysis, Sigmund Freud (1856-1939), offered a theory of religion in which religious experience can be seen as a form of projection. Freud claimed that religion springs from a feeling of helplessness coupled with the experience of childhood. The child is helpless and dependent upon the parent; the adult continues to feel helpless, and so projects a being upon which to be dependent. The Divine, on this account, is a 'parent-substitute' projected by the mind to evade insecurity. It may be argued, on the other hand, that humans are in fact dependent upon a divine entity which commands love and respect, and this is why emotions such as love and respect are associated with dependency on one's parents. If the argument is turned around in this way, God is no longer a parent-substitute: parents are 'God-substitutes'.

But is there any evidence to suggest that religion, and religious experience, arise from projection? One possible piece of evidence is the similarity between the language used by mystics, for example, and that used by psychotics. Psychotics fail to recognise inner mental disturbances for what they are, and so project them onto the outer world, thereby seriously misperceiving their situations. This is manifested in their use of situation-descriptive language to refer to events that are, in fact, purely psychological: a psychotic may say "I am not real any more", when the statement "I have a feeling of unreality" would be more appropriate. Mystics also use situation-descriptive language, such as "I was merging into the One", rather than psychologically-descriptive language, such as "I felt as though I was merging into a greater unity". The similarity between mystical language and psychotic language may be taken as evidence that mystics, like psychotics, are projecting inner mental events onto the outside world.

This, however, merely hints that mystical experiences may be states of mind. If mystical experiences are states of mind, this still does not show that they are not veridical. Take persecution complexes as an example. An individual may believe that she is being persecuted when there is no reason to think that this is so. Another individual who *is* being persecuted may have all the same feelings, and express them using similar language. States of mind, therefore, may be elicited by objective states of affairs: just because some people confuse inner disturbances with outer situations, it does not follow that such situations never occur or can never be perceived correctly.

It may be argued that some religious experiences, especially conversion experiences, are psychologically-based solutions to emotional crises. William James (1842-1910) considered conversion experiences to be a radical rearrangement of psychic energy around a new centre of interest, arising from unease about the previous centre of interest. According to Karl Marx (1818-1883), for example, religion is simply an illusory consolation sought by the economically and politically exploited. According to other thinkers, the crisis that gives rise to religion need not be economic or political. Some philosophers, such as Jean-Paul Sartre (1905-1980), have claimed that the individual is abandoned to a life that is meaningless unless the individual gives meaning to that life. A conversion experience, given this understanding of life, is an attempted escape from the responsibility for giving life meaning, by seeking a ready-made meaning of life. Such an analysis seems to accord well with Tolstoy's conversion experience (see pages 13-14). Conversely, however, it may be argued that life *is* meaningless without the correct relationship with the Divine, and that Tolstoy and others like him have discovered this truth which Marx and Sartre either failed to notice or refused to acknowledge. (Freud, Marx, and Sartre were all convinced atheists before constructing their respective philosophies.)

It may be that religious experiences are simply invasions of the unconscious into consciousness. Freud considered there to be unconscious desires and wishes, impulses that have been repressed by consciousness due to the fact that they might occasion disapproval. The unconscious is not normally accessible to consciousness, according to this theory, so an unconscious impulse invading consciousness might be mistaken as the voice, or guidance, of another entity. Furthermore, since my unconscious is in fact part of me, the 'other entity' that these impulses may be understood as arising from might be experienced as united in some sense with me. The 'Yorkshire Ripper', Peter Sutcliffe, who murdered at least thirteen women, claimed to have heard a divine voice urging him to kill these women. This may be an example of repressed wishes being mistaken for the guidance of another.

This account of religious experience, however, does not explain why unconscious desires may suddenly invade consciousness. Whilst it

31

may sometimes be due to random chance or psychosis, it is not entirely implausible to suggest that it may sometimes be due to divine agency. That is, even if a religious experience can be linked to the unconscious, it does not follow that the religious experience is not veridical: the Divine entity may be at work using the unconscious as a tool.

Finally, it has been proposed that some religious experiences may be due to the power of positive thinking. It may be supposed that wished-for events or states of affairs may come about by virtue of a positive attitude towards them. For example, if a person has a positive attitude towards the possibility of getting a certain job , he or she is likely to look for and find the relevant vacancies, and to be positive in application letters and interviews; a negative attitude towards the same object may result in that person not bothering to apply so often or not pushing forward his or her best characteristics in the application procedure. Positive thinking, then, can make a difference to the way events turn out. It has been suggested that perceived external answers to prayer are simply the result of the individual's positive attitude. A person's new-found contentment after a conversion experience, the argument runs, may also be accounted for in this way.

However, some religious believers claim that events have occurred, or situations have come about, for which they have prayed but about which they felt negative. That is, despite having prayed about a certain possible event, the religious believer may still feel that it will not occur, and be very surprised when it does. Moreover, religious believers also sometimes claim that their prayers have been 'answered' through the actions of other people, whom they may not even know. It is difficult to see how this could be an effect of positive thinking.

▶Is the origin of an experience relevant?

The above explanations of religious experience are only speculative and unverified. Furthermore, all psychological analysis presupposes certain philosophical principles that may be debated. However, these claims do seem to present a strong challenge to the claim that religious experiences are veridical. Some philosophers, such as William James, have argued that nothing that can be discovered about the origin of a religious experience can shed the slightest light on the spiritual value or significance of that phenomenon. This is certainly the view of the psychologist and psychedelic researcher Timothy Leary, whose article 'The Religious Experience: Its Production and Interpretation' (1963) begins:

> "Three years ago ... I ate seven of the so-called 'sacred mushrooms' which had been given to me by a scientist from the University of Mexico ... I was whirled through an experience ... which was above all and without question the deepest religious experience of my life."

There seems to be no philosophical or theological difficulty with the claim that a genuine religious experience may have a natural origin. Theistic religions claim that the Divine works primarily through natural phenomena, so to use and enhance human capabilities may simply be one method of divine activity. Also, theistic religions hold that humans are divinely created, so natural faculties that lead some to religious experiences may be designed precisely for that purpose. Pantheistic religions, on the other hand, hold that nature is at least an element of the Divine, and so again there is no problem with the notion that the Divine will may be manifested, or at least signalled, in natural occurrences.

Moreover, it does not seem as though the circumstances surrounding an experience can tell us anything about whether that experience is veridical. For example, if a person ingests some lysergic acid diethylamide (LSD), and an hour later exclaims "There is a face at the window!", the person may be hallucinating. On the other hand, there may be somebody looking in through the window.

Finally, 'abnormal' psychological or physical states may be partly responsible for a veridical experience that the person might not otherwise have had. Schizophrenics, for example, often notice minute details of their surroundings that other people do not notice; schizophrenia makes a difference to how the person perceives his or her environment, but the perceptions are usually veridical.

IS RELIGIOUS EXPERIENCE EVIDENCE OF THE EXISTENCE OF GOD?

Due to the differing understandings of similar religious experiences in different cultures, it seems that religious experience as such should not be taken as evidence in favour of a particular religion. That is, religious experiences are understood by some to be experiences of God, and by others to be visions of Brahman, for example. Moreover, it is difficult to understand how a religious experience might disclose all the attributes of its object. Mystical experience, for example, seems to be experienced as contact with the Divine, whatever that may be, rather than contact specifically with Allah, for example. Conversion and prayer experiences, similarly, are attested by followers of different religions. Religious experience, therefore, may provide evidence that there is a deity, or a Divine Reality, but not that this deity is the one spoken of by any particular religion.

The question of whether such evidence is provided by these experiences can be divided into two distinct questions: does a religious experience provide the person experiencing it with evidence of a deity?; and, do the religious experiences of some people provide other people with evidence of a deity? The latter question is, obviously, dependent upon the former: if an experience provides the subject of that experience with no evidence for the existence of its object, it cannot provide anyone else with this evidence.

There are theological and philosophical objections to the very idea of religious experience, especially mystical experience. (See pages 21-26). However, it seems that religious experience, like any other experience, should be subject to the principle of credulity: experience is usually veridical, therefore any experience should be accepted as veridical unless there is strong *evidence* (as opposed to *a priori* reasoning) to suppose that it is illusory. (See pages 26-27). Religious experiences, therefore, provide evidence for the existence of their object unless there is good reason to suppose that they are illusory.

34

As we have seen, physiological and psychological explanations of religious experience have been advanced. These explanations, even if they are true, do not necessarily show that religious experience is not veridical, but they do provide an obstacle to claiming that religious experience is evidence of some Divine Reality. This is due to a philosophical principle, introduced by William of Ockham (c.1285-1349), known as 'Ockham's Razor'. This is the principle that entities are not to be multiplied beyond necessity; if a religious experience can be accounted for in naturalistic terms without reference to any divine entity, then the experience does not provide evidence that there is such an entity. That is, if a non-divine factor is present and is sufficient to produce an effect, there is no reason to suppose that the effect discloses a divine entity. The question of whether religious experiences provide their subject with rational evidence of a Divine Reality, then, hinges upon whether any non-religious factors, such as those we have already considered, are present and are sufficient to produce the experience. The first stage in assessing this possibility is to assess the plausibility of any non-religious explanations.

The question of whether one person's claims of religious experience provide another person with evidence of a deity reduces to the question of the value of human testimony. In *The Existence of God* (1979), Richard Swinburne argues for a 'principle of testimony': in the absence of positive reasons for supposing that the person reporting an experienced event is misremembering, exaggerating, or lying, their testimony is sufficient reason to believe that the experience in question actually occurred. This is because:

> "Other things being equal, we [usually] think that what others tell us that they perceived, probably happened."

General reasons for mistrusting a person's testimony concerning purported events of divine origin is provided by David Hume (1711-1776), in the section 'On Miracles' of *An Enquiry Concerning Human Understanding*. Hume writes:

> "The passion of *surprise* and *wonder*, ... being an agreeable emotion, gives a sensible tendency towards the belief of those events, from which it is derived ... the gazing populace, receive greedily, without examination, whatever soothes superstition, and promotes wonder."

Not only is there the likelihood that those who testify would have believed in the event even if it did not happen, but it is also probable that such a person might be trying to deceive others:

> "what greater temptation than to appear a missionary, a prophet, an ambassador from heaven? ... Or if ... a man has first made a convert of himself ... who ever scruples to make use of pious frauds, in support of so holy and meritorious a cause?"

Testimonies concerning religious events, according to Hume, are unreliable because the person making the claim may have been deceived, or may be trying to deceive others to serve either themselves or their religion. Against this view is the observation of the Religious Experience Research Centre that people are hesitant to report religious experiences for fear of ridicule.

Although Hume's observations may cast doubt on some particular claims of religious experience, it seems unreasonable to suppose that every assertion of such an experience is of this nature. Many alleged religious experiences lead to conversion to a religion, and are claimed to have occurred by usually humble people of seemingly sound judgement. In short, it does not seem that Hume's observations of human behaviour warrant wholesale rejection of the possibility of believing the testimonies of others concerning religious experiences.

It might be argued that reports of religious experiences are rather vague and disagree with one another over the content of such experience, and so there is no reason to suppose that such experiences really do occur. However, there is much similarity between reports of religious experiences, and many of the differences can be put down to the differing cultures of the subjects of the experiences. Furthermore, the vague language used to describe these experiences may be a necessary product of the nature of the experiences —uncommon and often ineffable. Languages grow to suit the purposes of their communities, and describing religious experiences is hardly a primary concern of any linguistic community. It is hardly surprising that such experiences cannot be precisely described using natural languages.

It seems, then, that it is rational to accept the testimony of another person that a religious experience has occurred, unless there are specific reasons to mistrust the particular person reporting the event (e.g., the witness is known to be a pathological liar). The question of whether religious experience provides evidence of a deity reduces to the question of whether naturalistic, or non-religious, observations are sufficient to explain the origins of these experiences.

EXAM QUESTIONS

Since it is important to answer the question set, the key terms of the question (e.g., 'revelation') should be defined at the beginning of the essay and used throughout. It is also helpful to give examples to clarify these definitions. Questions on **revelation** are usually fairly straightforward, requiring an understanding of the two views of revelation and a critical discussion of them. The question may refer to these views using terminology you have not encountered, so be clear about the concepts involved and you should recognise them whatever guise they are in. Questions on **religious experience** are more varied. Since some areas of discussion are relevant only to particular types of religious experience, it is particularly important to be selective: there is no time to discuss everything that is relevant to the question. Consider the following examples:

Is Revelation divine communication to humans, or human discovery of the Divine?

Definitions: 'Revelation'.
Divine communication: propositional view.
Human discovery: nonpropositional view.

Criticisms of each view. Assessment.

How far are Religious Experiences open to nonreligious interpretations?

Definition of 'Religious Experience';
examples: prayer, mysticism, conversion.
(each explained briefly).

Mysticism and neurophysiological explanation:
hallucination due to drugs, electricity, brain tumour, tuberculosis.

Conversion and psychological explanation:
Freud; Marx; Sartre; positive thinking. (e.g.: Tolstoy.)

Origin and spiritual value: James.

WORKSHEET

1. Which view of revelation is implied by each of the following claims? Justify your answer.
   (a) "The world is charged with the grandeur of God" (Gerard Manley Hopkins)
   (b) "Faith is the assent to any proposition not made out by the deduction of reason but upon the credit of the proposer" (John Locke)
   (c) "revelation ... is only a description of one of the signs of faith" (Leo Tolstoy)
   (d) "Faith has no merit where human reason supplies the truth" (St. Gregory the Great)

2. Are the propositional view of revelation and the nonpropositional view of revelation mutually exclusive? Justify your answer.

3. Give three common features of religious experiences.

4. What are the major characteristics of the following types of religious experience?
   (a) Conversion.
   (b) Mysticism. (Distinguish *introvertive* from *extrovertive* types).
   (c) Prayer. (Distinguish *internal* from *external* responses).

5. A. The taste of a good curry.
   B. Fear whilst watching a horror film.
   C. A dehydrated desert traveller's hallucination of an oasis.
   D. A dream.
   E. An extrovertive mystical experience.

   (a) Which of the above experiences are 'ordinary'?
   (b) What do you think it means to call an experience 'ordinary'?

6. Give examples of everyday experiences which are:
   (a) Ineffable.
   (b) Noetic.
   (c) Transient.
   (d) Passive.

7. A. Seeming to see text.
   B. Seeming to see a ghost.
   C. Seeming to hear voices.
   D. Seeming to hear a car engine.
   (a) For each of the above experiences, say whether an explanation can be given of the experience without reference to the object as existing independently of the mind.
   (b) If such an explanation can be given, does this necessarily mean that the object does not exist independently of the mind?

8. A. "I have felt the presence of ghosts."
   B. "I have met the Prime Minister."
   C. "I have seen this planet from the moon."
   D. "I was once abducted by beings from another planet."
   For each of the above claims, say whether:
   (a) You would believe a stranger who made such a claim.
   (b) There is a strong chance that the claimant is lying.
   (c) There is a strong chance that the claimant is deluded.
   (d) It is possible that your reaction might mislead you.

9. Can a person's claim to have had a private experience be verified? If so, how?

10. A question from Sigmund Freud: "If the truth of religious doctrines is dependent on an inner experience that bears witness to the truth, what is one to make of the many people who do not have that experience?"

FURTHER READING

Revelation

C. Stephen Evans. *Philosophy of Religion: Thinking About Faith.*
(IVP: 1982)
Readability: * * * Content: #
Chapter 5. Not very critical.

J. Hick, *The Philosophy of Religion.* 4th edn. (Prentice Hall: 1990).
Readability: * * * Content: ###
Chapter 5. A good survey of the area.

Avery Dulles, *Models of Revelation* (Doubleday: 1983).
Readability: * * Content: ####
A clear and detailed discussion.

Religious Experience

B. Davies, *An Introduction to the Philosophy of Religion.* 2nd edn.
(OUP: 1993).
Readability: * * * Content: ###
Chapter 7. Covers most of the issues in a straightforward way.

C. Stephen Evans. *Philosophy of Religion: Thinking About Faith.*
(IVP: 1982)
Readability: * * * Content: ##
Chapter 4. Makes good use of models of experience.

Alister Hardy, *The Spiritual Nature of Man: A Study of Contemporary Religious Experience.*
(Clarendon: 1979; reprinted by Mulberry/Alister Hardy Society: 1992)
Readability: * * Content: ###
A modern and scientific study of religious experience, based upon surveys carried out in the 1970s.

William James, *The Varieties of Religious Experience: A Study in Human Nature.* (Fontana: 1960).
Readability: * * Content: ####
Written from the viewpoint of a psychologist, this is the first major study of religious experience, and remains a classic.

J. L. Mackie, *The Miracle of Theism: Arguments for and against the existence of God*. (Clarendon: 1982).
Readability: ** Content: ##
Chapter 10. Good for an atheist's perspective.

R. Swinburne, *The Existence of God*. Rev. ed. (Clarendon: 1991).
Readability: ** Content: ##
Chapter 13. Detailed analysis of experience in general and a defence of the principle of credulity.

A wide range of research materials, including books, pamphlets, and audio cassettes, are produced by the Religious Experience Research Centre and can be obtained through:
The Alister Hardy Society, Westminster College, Oxford, OX2 9AT

KEY   Readability   * manageable;   ** good;
                                   *** very good;   **** excellent.

             Content   # adequate;   ## good;
                                   ### very good;   #### excellent.

GLOSSARY

Fides—'Faith' in the sense of intellectual assent to a set of propositions. For example, faith that God created the universe.

Fiducia—'Faith' in the sense of trust and commitment. For example, faith in the Prime Minister.

Heilsgeschichte—'Holy history': the period of history recorded in the Bible, from the origins of the nation of Israel to the birth of the Christian community.

Ineffable—Something that cannot be suitably expressed in words.

Natural theology—The use of reasoned argument to assess basic religious claims, such as the existence of God.

Noetic—An experience is noetic if it contains information.

Object of experience—The thing which is experienced, even if the experience is not veridical.

Pantheism—The belief that humanity and nature are elements of an all-inclusive divinity.

Passive—An experience in which the subject of the experience contributes nothing. The opposite of 'active'.

Subject of experience—The person having the experience. For example, the mystic is the subject of a mystical experience.

Theism—The belief in a single omniscient and omnipotent personal deity, creator of everything else that exists and distinct from that creation.

Transient—Brief or fleeting, rather than permanent or durable

Veridical—An experience is veridical only if the object of the experience exists as it is experienced, within the subject's field of experience. For example, I may experience seeing a chair. This experience is veridical only if there is a chair in front of me that matches the one in my experience.

NOTES